BEFRIENDING SHADOWS

Poetry

ASHLEY LYNN

COPYRIGHT

The poems in this book were written from the author's experiences with certain groups, ideologies, and hardships.

First paperback edition October 2024

Book design by Ashley Lynn
Cover design by Ashley Lynn
Cover font Chocolate Box by Paul Floyd

ISBN: 978-1-7342121-8-1
E-book ISBN: 978-1-7342121-6-7

Published by Adventures Across Press
adventuresacross@protonmail.com

Ashley Lynn

To my love
Thank you for walking with me in the forest

To all of the old souls who struggle with these interesting times
I see you

TABLE OF CONTENTS

THE CRISIS   11

Into the Dark Woods 73

BEFRIENDING SHADOWS   117

TOGETHER, OUT OF THE WOODS   151

START HERE

This collection is a journey through a dark forest segmented into four parts:

THE CRISIS of disorientation: I attempted to leave society behind and exit the matrix by starting my own platform around spirituality and content creation, adopting negative lifestyle patterns that isolated me from my loved ones and the common folk. All of this was done to protect myself from the world around me, my past hurts, and my sensitive nature. The crisis was the stage when I realized I was stuck and couldn't live like this anymore.

INTO THE DARK WOODS of my anger and shame: I had to face the cauldron of suppressed emotions I accumulated while trapping myself in my bubble, and how that affected my life and relationships. Facing my inner darkness took courage and bravery, each day something new revealed itself and I opened up to what appeared. There was no more hiding, I had to walk through the dark woods and listen to every bit of shame, pain, fear and hurt inside of me.

BEFRIENDING SHADOWS of accepting who I am, my past, and the world around me: I made friends with my shadow self and found empowerment while shedding my old self.

TOGETHER, OUT OF THE WOODS of finding hope & healing for the future: By the end of the journey, I accepted what happened and who I became. This is the beginning of coming back to myself and what I truly am in my heart - the "why" I create. We leave off on a clean slate, a glimmer of who I am outside of the dark woods and realizations of how I can move forward with an attitude change.

I wrote these poems as I went through my Dark Night of the Soul. For me, it was like walking into a dark forest looking for the lost parts of myself and bringing them back into my life. Each poem is like another shadow I encountered during the quest of reclaiming myself.

WHAT'S WITH THE ITHERS?

As humanity moves onward through this century, we rely on the internet for sustaining our lives in many ways. We all use the internet for entertainment, social interactions, schooling, research, news. You name it, we need it.

Ithers (pronounced *ee-thers*) is a word I made up to talk about the internet, especially social media. The internet is like a field of consciousness that surrounds us. It contains all information, ever. Well, most of the information we know of.

Ither is a man made version of an invisible realm, perhaps like a spirit realm, containing within it the impurities of man as well as the good. In a way, the *ithers* are alive and seems to have a sentience of its own.

Several times in this book I use the word *Ithers* to describe the internet. I battled the internet, specifically social media, and finding a balance was challenging to say the least.

By the end of creating this book, I had to learn how to have a healthy relationship with the internet. I love the *ithers* and all I can do online. Fully giving up the internet would be difficult for me, even though I write about the ideal of living without it in some of my poems. Removing the internet from our lives is idealistic to think about but perhaps we can find ways to make it more enjoyable and healthier for *everyone*.

I hope through my poetry collection, I can inspire you to create a healthier relationship with the internet, however it looks for you. The internet is so intertwined in our daily lives nowadays, but perhaps you will feel motivated to seek out more in our physical reality for there are so many opportunities out there for you.

Much love,

Ashley

Befriending Shadows

THE CRISIS

// Disorientation //

\\ The world is upside down and I am floating sideways //

THE ART OF BEFRIENDING SHADOWS

I asked for creativity
The muses
They brought me
In front of my worst enemy

Evil, she rattled
In the cage I kept her in
I wanted to be the best to everyone
Inside
She ate at my skin

I called upon creativity
For a way out of this
"The way out,
Is through - you know what ye must do"
And shook the cage
To get her rattlin'

Thoughts, she cried
Constantly in my mind
Not knowing who my opponent is
A war against myself

What I didn't know
Together, we are whole

This isn't what I want to do right now
My destiny, a bright light awaits me
Raging emotions
Inside did stir
From traumas new and old
Unable to heal & be heard

"All I need to do
Is give her a voice
And let her choose
'There's a way to get along"

Poetry poured
From my fountain tip pen
Again and again
Unwinding
My terrorized mind
Clear seeing, once blind

As I let her out of the cage
More and more rage
Came along the path
Once calmed and relaxed
My, she's not that bad

The merging has begun

As she spoke more and more
An enemy, she became not
But a sister
Sinister things happened to her
She became a fiery volcano

The more we merged
The more powerful I emerged
And years and years of guilt
Unlayered the grip around us
Feeling trapped, dissolved at last

And now we have a book
To tell our tale

WILL SOMEONE APPROACH ME?

I always desired
In social settings
Sitting alone
Lonely in the corner
Twiddling my thumbs
Looking into other corners
The desert wanderer within
For others to approach me
And invite me in
In to whatever they were doing
The desire to be invited
Included
Belonging
I always desired

Here I sit
Waiting for someone to approach me
In my "old age"
Yet no one ever comes
And they never will
Being left out isn't done intentionally
Maybe others believe I want to be solitary
So they leave me be
How can anyone know I'm lonely
If I don't say a thing?

Of course, it's obvious
If I want attention
I need to seek it
Ask for it
Engage myself with others
Being invisible is natural for me

But being seen?

ℐNVOLUNTARILY Sᴏʟɪᴛᴀʀʏ

My weakness is love
        Is resonance
                With the above

I fall so easily
        I mistake it for destiny
                On the other side I see so clearly

        What does the woman do
Fully and her beauty
        her purity
        her wisdom
        her intellect

With a wound of being involuntarily solitary
        and attracting men
                who would gobble her up
                      and suck her dry

Like a stolen selkie from the sea
        yet I here remain free
            and see
                    their starstruck eyes
                        searching for me

I will find my selkie sisters
        for now I must turn away
                one cannot have room for Grace
        if darkness and deceit are in her place

ORDINARY

Sometimes I hate being so sweet
So normal, so ordinary
When what I want is to be extraordinary

Unique
A tulip in an onion field
The center of attention

I want crowds to look at me
Join me, be an essence, together
My creativity so ordinary

I want a way to let my uniqueness out
Free
For everyone to see

Its not that I'm scared or stuck
Its more of, I'm too logical
Unoriginal

I can't even copy the ones I admire most
Trying so hard to be original
But it's so boring, my ordinary-ness in the way

Like an academic book
The same thing everyone has to read
Math, history, science

Where's my creative edge?

I look to others for inspiration
I hate comparing my self
But I do

Because I feel like I've failed
In creating things new and totally original
Unusual, eye catching, phenomenal

PAST

The past is a parasite
Reminiscent of a ghost pipe
Siphoning life
From mycelium
What strife

WRITE

I desperately want to write again
Yet it's been so long since I wrote you
Where do I even begin?
Where did I leave off?
Starting again feels awkward
Should I even do this again?
Should I leave it in the dust?

The urge, the desire
To write from my heart
As she wants to speak freely
But feels like she's been wrong
Did wrong. said wrong
Because everybody is gone

Has she actually? - No
She's always growing
Doing her best
And in this rest
Found out it's all been a test
For evolving
Even if it's like turning to ashes
To start once again

Seems fitting
Since my name is Ash

So maybe I will write again
Even though I'm scared
Scared more of myself
Judging myself before anyone else can
Like it'll protect me from being hurt again
I'm so sensitive
Maybe I should be nicer to myself
So I don't hurt my own feelings

I'm allowed to be
Do
Think
Say
Anything I want
And if I come from an integral heart
I can do no harm

People might not like me
How could we love everybody?
Only in moderation, I say dotingly
I must allow myself to speak freely
A writer must write
Even if no one reads it

I do hope someday people will read my writing
How could one do a profession
Vocation
If no one is receiving it?

Millennial Mycelium

Generations of people are archetypal
Millennials, a unique one indeed

Millennial mycelium
Personally, a delirium

People before us didn't mean to do it yet
We're here processing trauma from hundreds of years ago

Many of us are here
Of course to spread cheer

But to also find compassion for those who came before
And lived survivally, year after year

We alchemize the old ways to new
Continuing on from a place of love

Instead of struggle
Or waiting to get to above

It's up to us to make life paradise
We shan't wait till we retire

We decompose the old ways, the lies
And turn them to soil, for new generations to thrive

We have a lot of work to do
We have weight on our shoulders

From the mistakes of our ancestors
Yet in paradigm time, there are no mistakes

Will we ever get anywhere?
Rising prices make it hard to climb

Yet mycelium fungi do climb
Up the towers of rotting old paradigms

And bloom high
Into the canopies

Yet most of us
A consciousness network

Learning new human perks
Dig ourselves deep in the ground

The communication systems
For trees, roots, hibernating bees

Telepathy, speaking
Without words

High pitched frequencies
Like the birds

I'm not sure what's next
How could the world possibly evolve more?

What I do know, we'll emanate nature
And decompose forevermore

THE BURNING FEAR

This fear I have
The fear of being seen
Comes not of what they say about me
But the silence cast in blank stares

This fear I have
The fear of being seen
Comes from lives long gone
Living peacefully
The priestess, the witch, the magician
Amongst devas and ethereal spirits
Being hunted at the end of it
And killed, by being me

Even at the end of that life
I knew I'd be here again
Practicing the same beautiful techniques
In a forest den

Even then, as the mob took me away
I went on with a smile on my face
Knowing one day
People would cherish the Goddess again

The smile on my face
Knowing they are fools
For life as a soul is eternal
I'd live on after I died

This fear I have
The fear of being outed
All I want is to be understood
And not at all doubted

For I know the invisible is real
To experience it, one must feel
Perhaps, in time, the eyes will reveal
The higher dimensions, as veils peel

Not everyone is a seer
Mobs are quick to start a jeer
My fear
Of reputation gone peculiar
A whole community
Not able to see her

Perhaps in silence the true power resides
Externally quiet
Yet inside opens minds
A royal being I may be
Reflected within them
Themselves, to see
Once their inner mirror
Is clear

VICES, VICES, VICES

Vices Vices Vices
We all have our vices
All the shadow's choices

The shadow and the ego
Can be one and the same
They both desire trivial things
Money, power, sex, and fame

For me, my vices
Are being noticed on devices
To be seen! Huge!
In an ocean of many hues!

Being a child, my thoughts did conspire
Wanting validation from inattentive parents
And screaming for justice
From traumatizing wrongdoings

Why do I want fame?
To prove that I'm not lame
Ordinary, plain, when I know
That I'm extraordinary

Vices Vices Vices
I spend much of my time with vices
They block me from what's important
Off the devices

Vices Vices Vices
The only way to make them stop
The wifi wizard away on holiday
His magic boxes had died in weather-vain
And cannot fix them right away

Vices Vices Vices
I still try to do them!
Writing poetry about
All that is triggering

Is still giving the vices
Power over me
They only want to be seen

The reason "I" am not seen
Is because my
Vices Vices Vices
Keep me on a screen
Tell me I'm not serene
And that I shouldn't share
Their sneaky ways
Ashamed
Of being stuck
In vices

No-Reality

Nothing feels real anymore
     No matter the intention
Everyone's doing it for the
     Gram, money, fame, looks, criticism, cynicism

There's no getting away from it
     Is anything authentic?
Everyone's an expert
     At something
Yet no one knows anything
     But why does that even matter?
Is anyone doing it for the pleasure?
     Without a reward?

I want to feel alive doing something
     Without the need for a reward
        Without having a reward
     For the reward makes me feel
        Less real

Because it's what I want so bad that I would sacrifice
Quality, authenticity, integrity
     To get it

Making simple decisions gets harder
     Am I doing it because my heart wants it?
     Or because it'll get me some reward?
Is this for pleasure,
     Does it support my self love?
     Is it guidance from my soul above?

Synchronicities help me decide
     Logic confirms, the easy ride
And then it's decided, that yes, it's destined

I move along my path
     With distractions all over the map
        I'll always find my way,
           My soul, I've not to pay

Money Poems

Why do I think I
Can make money from my emotions?
Often in inner commotion
When I have such notions

Books I'll write
About my emotions
My shadows
The words pour out

Honestly, I can't help it
Writing is a vice
A vice, perhaps?
Or one of my talents?

My mind gets caught in a tangle ball of confusion
Why, oh why, should I make money from my emotions?!

WILL YOU SPREAD THE WORD?

I put my faith into you
Why, you offered to me
To spread the word about
My musings, me choosing,
To give my power to you

When it turned blue
And crickets mocked me in my ears
It was you I resented
For failing me for years

I wait to be discovered
Above the world, I hover
No one can see me
Why should I blame thee?

A fear to share
Is it a fear? Or a delay
From me, my higher self
To wait deary dear
Until the coast is clear?

Ashley Lynn

INFORMATION AGE

Chatter crunches the space around me
      Advice from every which way
          Mind you, no delay

For discernment,
      You? Can I trust?
          No, trash that

Everything I hear is a truth,
      But truth to me?
          I fail to see

It takes too much time to process
      Than to keep on swiping
                Swiping
                  Swiping
        So I trust
           Even if I bust

CONTENT ONLINE

I realize
                              I despise
          Watching content
                Online

What happened
          To the thrill of seeing a movie?
                                        Pondering for a few days
                To truly grasp the meaning?

          What about visiting a crystal clear lake
So many pictures I'd take
                              Only to swim a minute or two
          My, the waters so deep and blue!

          Two weeks time lapsed, no internet at last

          The moment I can use again
                                   I'm disinterested
Disgusted even
                         That a gaggle of people
          Can do this for a living
                         Creating content

                                   Sure, it can pay
But it's feeding humanity's addiction
                                   Of moving away
                From harnessing life

VICE GRIP

Vice
That thing you're addicted to
Whatever it may be
Has a grip on you

Vice
Another word for addiction
A rendition of a common handyman tool
The one in your dad's basement

Both technically do the same
They keep something gripped
Though pressure on a rusty bolt
Is different than your brain
Shocked by an electric volt
Losing your way

ꟼRKSOME ꟼTHERS

It irks me that I continually
Work, work, work to be noticed
On the ithers

Like what I'm doing is
The new way, or some
Spiritual wisdom I got today

It irks me that I feel disappointed
Once projected, nothing is reflected
Crickets ring in my ears

Does my life not matter?

It irks me, that I continually follow fame
Could I even handle it?
If thousands of people knew my name?

What if I met with thousands of people someplace?
Surely, it'd be too much, so why am I wasting
My energy on such a disgrace?

It irks me, that my art isn't seen
Yet what I put out there
Is hardly my art

Just more reasons to
Love me, to see clearly
The shadows

I am loved, I'm truly loved! By people
Who are not meeting me in the ithers
Where our connection is reality not a fallacy

It irks me, that even after
Years, and years, and years
I'm still trying to be seen, noticed

Ashley Lynn

Have some fame for being Ashley
When all the skills and talents I have
Fall short to me to share with my audience

So I spend less time
Creating with them

It irks me, that I'm writing this poem
Still, my life's work goes unnoticed
And I'm here writing, bantering

About not being seen
When I don't even let people see me
For me

See me as a celebrity!

ITHER FAME

Today
Here I am today
Writing more poems
At my dismay...

You'd think by now
I'd have changed
I'm seeking
Fame
To validate
The path I decided to take
Unconventional, entertaining perhaps
Please watch me!
Fill with green bills, my chaps!

Genuinely, to take a slight turn
The way I live my life
Is what makes passion burn
My heart, it loves
The way I've chosen
My heart, I've followed
My soul no longer broken

Yet here I am
Irked at my own behavior
Needing to be my own savior
Ego desires become greater
Look at me! Look at the way I live!
My ego must be trying
To dig my grave

Once the ither is turned off,
My eyes open
And to myself
I scoff

Look at all the projects I've started
And left behind
Believing less in them
To strive
On the ither

They call it marketing
Social media
YouTube
Putting yourself online
Perhaps true
Yet first, I must find my sublime

Attention I did take,
Off the ither
To become a better
Caretaker for myself

SENTIMENTALITY

I don't know what it's going to take
For me to get through this
Finally,
Finally
I'm with people
Kind people
Loving
Friendly family
I'm holding back my sentimentality
Because loving people too much
Has made them leave
Or take advantage of me

My biggest dream
Is standing before me
So much at stake
Our new threads
Delicately placed
A wrong move could send you away
You're going away anyway
Might as well take a chance

In the moment I wish I could
Allow myself to fully express
Impress
You with the moments collected
Skills, my passion
Yet I feel shy
I'll hide my light
Nervous tension prevention
Please don't tease me
For my innocence and purity

"LOVE OTHERS IN MODERATION, I SAY!

LOVING TOO MUCH SEQUESTERS,
SMOTHERS THE HEART FLAME"

I Am Here

I am here, living a simple life in the trees
In my house of trees, a landscape of trees
I enjoy my life in reverie

I sit next to the metal hearth
Burning trees, wondering
Why nobody sees me

They see *her*, clearly living the same
lifestyle as I. *She's* showered with money
and attention for putting it online

But is *she* truthfully happy?
Living life isolated in the woods
As am I?

Yet I am content
My life outside the screen
I am content

Living romantically with my family
Making dangly dragon tooth necklaces
Painting star systems

My life isn't aesthetically perfect
As it "should be"
I'm a mess and a mixture of everything

I guess that means I don't fit in
How could I ever win without the perfect
aesthetic life for the internet?

Why do I envy girls like *her*?
She's surrounded by material possessions
Receives loads of attention

Money falls into *her* lap
Hell, maybe *she* even sells herself
Is *she* even real?

Ah, another fallacy
And I know *she's* all alone

A million trees can never make up for
The dozens of people who could physically love *her*
Does *she* have any true friendships?

Or merely Instagram favorites?
She has to travel 1,000s of miles
To have a friend sleepover

Why do I envy *her*,
When I am already rich as me?

I want to be like *her*, my ego turning
I want to be successful, I'm sick of yearning
I want to see my work... Seen

Seen... in the hands of genuine love
I want my finances to be taken care of
Easily by people watching screens

It seems like everyone else is doing it
So why not me?

ARROGANT SPIRITUALIST

Why does the spiritual community
In its attempt at unity and ascension
Provide rejection
To that of earthly culture?

They long to go back "Up there"
Where the air is clear
Spirituality the main purpose
For a being to embody divinity

Isn't the divine law
The will to create
All that makes up culture?
Humans are the greatest creators of all
Such diversity in the mind
Facets of Creator's mind

I'm a walking paradox
I can embody many opposites
Things I love and attract
Can seemingly contradict

Yet I can be a divine vessel
Of universality
By allowing myself to be
One
And to openly show up
With a loving heart
To all the artists and creativists
Sharing what they see in themselves

Ascenders wince their eyes
With my punk cries
"Oh the distortion!
Oh what lies!
Oh darling,
Maybe someday you'll see
You'll understand
True divinity"

I say fuck you
For failing to see within you
That black moon rising
Medusa crying
The shadow feminine
She wishes not to cause destruction
But understanding
Of all facets of life

Purists, spiritualists fail to see
That the problems within society
Remain a flame within thee
A flame destroying the inner garden
Not because it is evil
But because it wants to be seen
And given a purpose
For expressing its divinity

New Age Tactics

When I thought I was done
Done with my shadows
Transmuted, they are
No longer holding me in the gallows

Wake up, I do
In the morning, sky blue!
A bright beautiful day!
What's that? A trigger at bay
A friend sends me some spiritual wooha
A woman who surely can read the akasha
And can upgrade your diamond body
Listen to her transmission
Programming a folly

Enraged I became!
Why is everyone insane?
Why do spiritual people fall victim
To another trapping tactic?

Within the answers always reside
Why do we always search online?
For what we truly desire
Inner connection
From our higher divine

We need not
Listen to others

Spirituality
Is relative to individuals
Teach the simple points
Leave the rest to personal imagination
Not a silly transmission

Nearsighted

Aren't we a bit nearsighted as a society?

Creating civilizations with chalk on driveways

Failing to notice

The impending rain storm forming in the distance

Our plans for the future

Silt on the bottom of a river

Physicality

One day I desired to leave the matrix
Surely, for my life? This was the perfect fix
The matrix was a trap, too much working!
Shackles that held me in grindstone mentality

So onward I went! Head full of dreams
I quickly learned the powers inside me
The ability of my thoughts creating reality
Was all I needed to know to set me free

So I quit my jobs, I stopped working!
And traveled around, minimal needs, nomadically
A lot of baggage, I carried inside
All too heavy for me to fly

Along my journey I lightened my load
Faced my fears! For me, so bold
Learned about the conscious universe
That within me, lost memories did stir

Inside awakened a higher perspective
Cosmic beings, within me, were reflected
Realizing we're also infinite, souls without boundaries
Many lives we've lived, each in a living library

Somewhere along my journey, I left Earth!
Forgot what it meant to, here, have worth
Sometimes a higher vibration is all it takes
To have purpose here, to make a change

A new desire I felt inside
To become physical, once again, and sway with the tides
The matrix felt like hopeless fate to me
But creating beauty in the physical is my destiny

THE ONLY WAY YOU CAN BE
TRAPPED BY THE DARK MATRIX IS
BELIEVING YOU ARE IN IT

BETRAY

The way you betray me
Doesn't cut like a knife

It feels like forgotten crystals upon a look-about rarely used
A moment together once placed there

A tender memory engrained in them
Remembered only by one

Surely life changes I get that
We must evolve to become more resilient to this world

Become stronger, yet
When exchanging pieces of soul to do that

And leaving treasures behind
For no other reason than

It becomes too much effort to try
Important elements get left behind

It takes two to tango
Life's dance goes by in a glance

Yet if life is a dance
Shouldn't it be more fun?

Whittling away on important matters
Instead of creating canvas splatters

Touching glass as if it'll bring a sense of wonder
When it keeps a vessel stagnant

In our universe we float apart

Hurt by sheer ignorance
Not the type of innocence

Disinterest can make one feel unimportant
My spark for life not able to spark yours

Does that mean it's all vanity?
Like being with me is a chore?

I know you love me, you tell me everyday
And that I'm beautiful

Yet actions speak louder
Than anything you say

I Hope She Quits

I hope *she* quits
Throws *her* "life" away
Because maybe
She'll live life a new way

I hope *she* quits
Because the pressure, the fallacy, the lost treasures
Get to *her*
And *she* finally realizes *she's* been living for lies

I hope *she* quits
And starts *her* life anew
One of a genuine hue
Where true friends can come through

I hope *she* quits
Because I can see it's killing *her*
To always have to perform
To always have to sell *her* body
To get attention
To get money

I hope *she* quits
So *she* can finally meet *herself*
The true definition of wealth

In spirit, there is no money
There is no "reward"
The payment is
Being able to soar

ADDICTIONS

Addictions, we all have them
Addictions, a part of the human plan

It takes true discipline
To overcome addictions
And keep them at bay
Once within them
Our choices fade away

My heart goes out to
Those in addictions
I have them too
Even though I have restrictions

Addictions are something
We can feel proud of
Yet under the pride
Resides

Shame

Who's to blame?
If not ourselves, who?
If ourselves, why?
Self blame, *cry*

Your tears, dry
Find your inner light
Addictions aren't you
They show you a passion inside of you
You are capable to do

Healthy addictions?
What, like running and yoga?
I find moderation is best.
Even if "good" is how you define it.

SERVITUDE

My purpose in life is to live for me
I'm no longer in charge of my destiny
How could I think I could control the wild?
Free & untamed from boundary like a child

Servitude is a trick by society
"Serve others and you will have purpose,"
When I tire, I realize these shady tricks
Built up in my mind as dense bricks

Is it our purpose for us to enjoy creation?
What a challenge that is, allowing such a vibration
I've been trained as a slave replacing purity of mind
Run by illusion that I'm running out of time

They say, "Pursue your passions to find purpose"
A mind polluter, my passions superfluous

Any time I aspire to create
I halt myself, asking why, what purpose?
            Are you doing it for attention?

I am angry because anything I create
Comes with thought of what posts to make
            explanations to stake
                        defenses to hate
And it's no fun anymore

I wish to fill my mind with peace
To move on
And to let go with ease

INNER CONFLICT

I need to find my strength again
My burning passion for life
Sorry for myself, a penniless artist
Who lost her zest for limes

I want to uplift people
Be a positive force
To be that
I gotta be that
Do that

I feel almost lazy
For giving up my craft
A break I said I was taking

It's been a long break
And here I am being hard on myself again
For the inner conflict

Spiraling
        And spiraling
                And spiraling

GHOSTING

Part of me likes receiving
Long letter conversations
From like minded folks
We share funny jokes
On the Ithers, sometimes... in letters
On a similar level we are
Reading the same books

Synchronicities show us
We're on the same frequency bus
Traveling along a similar road together
This is magic! How could it get better?

Deep, deep, deep
In the abyssal dark trenches we go
Sharing the vastness of our souls
Problems verbally exchanged
My mind, deranged
Were you brought to me,
Because I'm an answer for you?
And you for me?
Suddenly, I shift my mood

Answers indeed, I have insight for you!
Today, tomorrow, never ending blues
Continually feeding, your inner demons reeling
Triggering or healing?
Rescuing, it's the least I can do

Vampires awaken disguised as a maiden
Vices unwound, addictions unbound
Needing, needing, needing
More, more, more
Insight, for you are!
Wisdom forevermore!

My energy dwindles
I can't see out my own windows!
All I can see and hear

Is your mental chatter, your inner banter
Insecurities flash like demon bats
Hungry for more, more, more!
LOVE ME
More, more more!

Yet no! I cannot fall in this trap
I turned from my own life
An escape for that
Which is an illusion
Such inner confusion

I have to put my defenses up
A cloak of being tough
Inside I soften
To the words I hear less often

In my life I am content
Peace and stability keep my health wealth met
I am on my path, though time it will take
Successes beheld, a difference I make

I can't engage
A boundary I must hold up to you
Not personally, but for you!
Humans cannot fix each other
It is up to our inner mothers
To assist in evolution
Of our personal blueprints

Even if the temptation is strong
My heart I must protect
My love is sacred to me

And I know I am not wrong

SHAMED HAPPINESS

Why is it
That when I share my bliss
Any reason for happiness
Your attention goes amiss?

Why is happiness
Invisible
Inconceivable
Impossible
To the ones who we want to share that with?

My happiness
Brings me much sadness
When experienced alone

I feel like I must dim my light for you
To even have you listen

The ones I can share my happiness with
Are the ones I cannot see
But I know
They celebrate me

A Watchful Eye

Being with you
Makes me feel
Like I'm standing in my past

Seeing the darkness that engulfed me
When life went too fast

Now, I'm grown, living in my bliss
Yet I cannot share my world with you
The message completely missed

How to enjoy time with commoners
Who cannot see their divine power?
I see what they cannot
Yet in silence I remain
In self imposed shackles and chains

I love in ways that cannot be
Received
So I tag along in observer mode
Silently in grief

A priestess you are too
Veiled at the moment, unknown
A sister I stand by your side
My true identity, I must hide

One day you'll wake up to your essence
Away I'll go with my presence
As our purpose
Will be fulfilled

RESCUER

My heart aches when I'm around you
A love I give, unconditional
Knowing I'll never receive it back
Reciprocal

Moving on would for me suit
Though abandonment I wish on no one
I will do my best to be loyal to you
Even if inside I wish to run

I am saddened I'll never be understood
You can listen intently with a blank stare
Not knowing what it's like actually being there

If one day you see my truth
Would you be sad if I have to leave you?
It's not you I have to leave
Yet I must fulfill my destiny

Anger

Anger
It boils through my veins
The way
You look at me with appearance
Of innocence
Is actually a mask you wear
Of who you are underneath

I can't decide for sure
If your intentions are pure
Or if you think other things of me
Behind ice glazed eyes

Surely someone with a mask of a
Spiritualist
Would like everyone to think
They've figured it out

COLD DECEMBER

Is my memory skewed?
My mind unglued?
I can hardly remember you
And the years and years
We meddled on
Two friends so true

Memories you share
Was I even there?
I don't remember the days
Of laughter and sunshine rays

Why is my memory
Clouded with tragedy?
Why can't I remember
Anything other than a cold December?

Ashley Lynn

STUCK

All of who I am is stuck in the   *could*
How how how

Stick my head in the ground
In darkness I'm found

Am I asleep
Dreams
Float
Outside my reach
Could it ever be?

Bare trees
Skeletons
Shiver in the breeze
Like me
Empty

If Mother Awakens

It saddens me
That my one mother
May never
See who I am genuinely

She knew I was different
But tried to make me fit in
For pursuing my authentic truth
Would reign pain on me
In their world

I speak blips of my infinite nature
She changes her body stature
And listens keenly
In her mind feeling
That I'm speaking fantasy

But no! Don't you know?
We have the power to change the status quo
What I speak of is truth
Words for the soul, to soothe

Silently I dim my light
So maybe I'll be in her sight
Alas, my heart loudly breaking
Aching
For it's naturally so bright

In ethereal transportation
I have mention
Of a goddess mother

I call upon her to shower me in love
And immediately
A dimension I shift, higher octave above

Moving in another reality
One in positive mentality
Where the invisible become visible
Colors and symbols present at the shift

My true divine mother
Is always around
She's present in every sight and sound

Tender eyes she adores me so
She teaches me this, see others glow

I use this on my one mother and realize
The divine mother resides in her eyes

She, herself isn't aware of it yet
That she is divine too
From the Mother
She's not met

The Music Festival

I found myself
At a music festival
To see my favorite band

I thought I'd meet people
Make friends, dance hand in hand
With lovers of the same music as me

What I found, was completely the opposite
A psychedelic experience
Without ingesting any substance

As I walked in
Hundreds of eyes missed mine
Invisible, I quickly noticed

Nobody saw me
Alone, I did saunter
Sad, alone

Trying to pick it up from years ago
Like the lyrics
Of one of the band's songs

What opened up around me
Was the manifestation of
The shadows of society

Each group of shadows, a squad
Shadows identify with
The consciousness of their mind

Clearly I could see this "movement" or that
With each squad a different vibe
Making a different tribe

Different colors, letters
Ignoring everyone else
Every one stuck in a trap

Identifying
Identifying
With the trends

Identifying
Identifying
With what everyone else was doing

If they didn't join in, they'd be outcast
Imagine, being outcast in a group of outcasts!!
People won't last if they're always trying to impress

Alas, people I approached not
How could I speak
Without being shot at?

By words of defending, is what I say offending?
If I don't understand the
Emerging cultural norms?

I innocently don't understand
What is going on these days
An old soul I am, I understand the soul's ways

Why is it, people identify with victimhood?
Anything that makes someone else wrong
Gives them power to unleash their shadows

Into the streets on a rampage
Burning down buildings, demanding change
When the change can only happen within themselves

We are already free
Our choices set the stage
Yet, they don't see it's all an illusion

A manifestation of shadows
The reality of it is
We're always free

We can always be who we want to be
The shadows tell us otherwise
And tell us to separate and despise

After getting turned down for paying
Cash for a t-shirt, like physical money
Doesn't mean anything anymore...

I wandered, eyes open
Into the crowd
Sardined into blobs of groups

Floating tins of sardines
Some anchovies...
Tuna, even?

People I didn't understand
Nobody's eyes met mine
Even though I could hold their hand

Or slap an ass
Being shoulder to shoulder
Bumping each other

In a sea
Of fleshy insanity
I guess I don't fit in a can

Somehow I felt
That this was a manifestation
Of the internet, Instagram

Ashley Lynn

Instead of scrolling my fingers
I scrolled my eyes and felt the
Overwhelming noise of shadows

As the crowd turned to waves
I bumped along, hands in the air
Together, we didn't care

Connection with each other
We had not, rare did I see
Other groups talk or share

Connection through lyrics
Wasn't even enough to
Greet each other

How could all these people
Who loved the same music
Walk around like they're the only ones there?

For others, they didn't care
Even though their Instagram profile
Says they do

Identifying with music
With lyrics, repeatedly speaking
The same thing over and over

Creates beliefs about oneself
The pit of a peach has it's toxicity
Cyanide eating away at the mind

By the end of it I felt disappointed
Craving human connection
Perhaps even a little inspiration

Left me feeling hollow
Like driftwood lost at sea
Floating on top of deranged society

A death, I experienced as tears
Fell from my eyes at the show
I didn't belong here, my light glowed

Invisible, I was resonating in another
Dimension, my understanding so different
That it made me invisible

I pushed myself between
Dozens of sticky, gelatinous bodies
Glue, almost, a way to suck me in

Stone cold in summer heat
Knowing this wasn't for me
This whole music scene

Illusion became my reality
For the last years
Identifying with someone else's songs

Sadness, loneliness sinking in
Deeper, and deeper, and deeper
To a sense of victimhood, perpetually alone

The illusion I witnessed around me
At the music festival
Was me

I was screaming to the wrong crowd
Who couldn't even see me, trying to
Reach those who seem most hurt

Yet completely unwilling to
Open and heal
The fuckery of society

I've been shouting to the rooftops
Hoping they'd hear me
Hear me say

"There's a better way!
Come, this way!
We can heal and create healthier ways!"

People won't hear me if they're
Not even listening to themselves
And their dying hearts

So, what now? My old ways
Ways I found in younger days
Instead of conforming to the norm

I must go down this path again
Lonely, I can think it is
Yet, along the path I always meet souls

Who do see me, love me
Even if they don't stay, they
Still love me and want me

As I want
Myself

CANYON EDGE

Toes dangle off
        The precipice,   the edge
                                          I made it to a dead end

Eyes gaze
        Down,
        down,
        down
                The canyon
                A haze hangs
                Above the river
                A mile deep

I made it here, scraping
        My two feet beneath me
Trudging through treachery
        Believing
        I'd arrive in my dreams
        Yet here I stand in
        Desolate misery

Is this a joke?
        Never
        ending
        relenting

                                          I was positive seeking
                                        But now I'm reeking
                                        Of failure, self-pity

I'm weak from trying
Crying, surviving
Thinking my toils
Were for thriving

                                          I am at this canyon edge
                                        Wondering if I'm dying

ℱAITHFUL Apps

Put your faith in yourself
Not in an app, who cares
If you're seen only by 10%
Of your followers?

Do it for yourself, because really?
You're the only one that matters
To you
Whatever you do
Acknowledge your own hands
People will never
Wait on the band stands for you
If you're begging them to

URGENT MESSAGE

// begin

Hello dear friend // a message to you I send
An invitation, perhaps // an open chance

Forces upon us // are creating confusion
A message I must // relay to you in trust

False light is littered // all over the ithers
Eating precious souls // greedy for gold

Protect your-self // you are full of wealth
Go within for wisdom // read books with the seasons

These people online // who claim to guide
Are not of the light // are they "real" in your sight?

Sources of media // mainstream, or social
Are the culprits of mania // in the physical, a "no show"

My invitation to you // turn off the screens, go green
Meet with your families // use your wisdom to see

Don't "follow" anyone // chase love to share the heart
Influencers on social media // are paid off from the start

The elders in your community // understand true unity
Authentic identities // can't be bought by companies

Be with ones you love // embrace with a hug
Seek long term satisfaction // friends, lovers, to share passion

Clear your mind // of the chaos online
Nature's fully open // a classroom, to soak in

All the wisdom you need // is within you, my dear
Ask your questions in silence // answers come in clear

Ashley Lynn

Until the ither becomes clear // from deception and fear
Be open to the real world // the coast will be clear

My wish for you // is to be sovereign and true
It can be hard to do // stuck in glue

Going green, it seems // is living with minimal screens
Experience your senses // hug trees, leave your defenses

I cannot save you, friend // you must wake up!
This message I send // to prevent humanity's end

// end

Befriending Shadows

INTO THE
DARK WOODS

\\ Anger \\

\\ I face my anger, rage & shame around the paradigm I
found myself in //

How Do You Identify?

Can we relate?
Without causing an inner debate?
Do I actually feel that way too?
Or am I trying to resonate with you?

Sieve, not sponge

Watch the words roll off my tongue

Exist?

I want to exist
To be here,
Yet expectations persist

I want to merge with the intelligences
- and experience -
What it's like being them

Why is it
That we're not allowed to just exist?
Why must we put on costumes
And play a part in a grand matrix?

I insist
We all stop and rest
Share a wave of consciousness
Among an eagle's nest
And glance
Upon something to the heart
That matters

Ashley Lynn

INSANITY

If you love something so much
Make it into your living
So that
Every day
You are giving
Giving
Giving
To yourself
And to humanity
That which soars your soul
Out of insanity

And you will never live a day
Regretting
Letting
Your life fly by
Unconsciously

STOP FEEDING THE SYSTEM

I am angry
    at all you're projecting
        intellecting
            conceptualizing
                analyzing
You're planting seeds
    caring for ill timelines
        with your thoughts and warnings
    destruction destroying
When it's all an illusion

I believe in abundance
    enough for all
        the power of nature
            the goddess call

Yet you project
    you protect
        a failing system
            held without wisdom

I say let it burn!
    To each other we shall turn
        And grow grass roots deep
    For a regenerative future
Our rewards we will reap

Seeds of fear
    Were planted back several years
        Anyone's thoughts and emotions of fear
            Support the growth of a timeline

Who were the farmers of the seeds?
    Why, the ones who want to control thee
        They know the truth of sovereignty
            Your divine right always available to be

They planted the seeds knowing
    The fruit would keep you from growing,
      From knowing
    The truth in your being
You are divine ever evolving

They know if you don't grow
    they run power over you
      the seeds of lies
        cause ethereal cries
      of timelines that are illusions

So dear one
    divine being from the stars

Will you drop the act and come join me?
    to fulfill your destiny
      of creating a new Earth
        A new humanity
      honoring femininity
    with nature and harmony?

HEART OPENING HUMANITY

Swimming in an ocean of insecurity
An ocean of fighting
Not directly, no

Mentally, with each other
Always believing
We're separate to each other

Always needing, defending,
And defeating. A war within society
A war within humanity

This war doesn't use guns and bombs
Terrorists, armies, because these days,
The war is with each other on the streets

Words hurt most
With the rise of sensitivity
And heart opening humanity

Each of us expanding
Evolving
Hell, maybe even "ascending"

Yet some of us confuse shadows
With reality and hang onto them
With animosity

DISCERNMENT

I'm angry at my naivety
My heart, my soul!
It trusts everybody

Innocent, until proven guilty
Though proving guilty
Isn't the first task for me

It takes time to get to know one
It takes time to see people's flaws
To discern if a person is good for me

On the Ithers, sometimes it's clear
That "seer?" sees the potential
In your wallet

Other times, it's not easy to see
Glitters and gold cover it up
There's fallacy

What's on the screen
Is meant for trajectory
Into their bank account

Is what they're saying true?
Is it wisdom that can help you?
Do they follow what they preach too?

Soul suckers, I like to call them
They rely on your attention
Without you they'd suffer, no direction

Within I, I see too
That this behavior
Is part of the human hue

Moments I feel this energy
Take over, a hypocrite I'd be
To deny this in me

I once followed
A fellow spiritual sister
An online "community leader"

Penniless farmer, I was working
Day and night growing organic food
For community lovers and foodie shovers

My body ached everyday, I was happy,
My toils did pay, in the "matrix?" I was not rich
Yet vast amounts of abundance filled my soul

Her wisdom so dear, sister she was to me
I thought she felt the same
To her, I was plain

I spent all my money on her course,
Life changing she claimed,
As money rolled into her bank

Books are cheaper, I could definitely learn more
By following my intuition
And building my spiritual core

I wish to rob her of the pleasure
Of receiving dollar bills
For exchange of fortune tales

Yet here am I trying the same
Telling stories on YouTube
Yet, me? Not in vain

Her spiritual group I joined
Spiritual truths were coined
I attended every Ither call, I saw and heard it all

She must have detected my interest in her
A fellow YouTuber, surely, enough to be a friend
Yet, wary of me, undercover again

Things felt wry when to the group, she let out a cry
"We wouldn't need gyms or to work out anymore!
If we grew our own food, worked in the fields until sore!"

Wait a minute, I thought, she never
Lifted a finger in a field - my job, could she yield?
I think not, my discernment reeled

Eventually I moved!
My plans were such anyway
Before giving into her ither fame

And all that she claimed
To the same town as she
She advertised online

In her videos, an experience sublime
Talking about the benefits of this and that,
Living in this town would provide a spiritual crown

Vortexes, earth energies alive, a place of
Crossing many Ley lines, gridworker I was,
Before I realized a facet of my truth, not ready to die

I moved there and lived in a tent, it was my
Highest excitement to live in this spiritual town
The land, enchantment abounds

This land became my second home
A place I didn't need my phone
To tell me spiritual truths

I found them within, without any brutes
Her I needed not anymore
For my soul to go on and soar

Penniless and poor I remained
That was okay, I wasn't looking for fame
Yet, she was and acted like royalty

Meeting her was a challenge
And once I did,
I felt betrayed

What was on the screen wasn't her at all
Sure, she ate only plants, meditated
Everyday, her aura, I admit, did radiate

Yet she projected so strongly
To stay out of the matrix, this
Town was a dystopian matrix

Civilization thrived on high paying
Dollar signs, spiritual quests,
Anything you'd see on the net

All for the consumerist purpose
Functioning better?
Or as another matrix?

Next thing I knew she sold out
She bought a house and added it
To the 3000 Bnbs overtaking the town

A friend in me? She saw not
Every time at the grocery store
Her vibes, awkward, fraught

Attention? Friendship?
Disappointing to me
She wanted nothing to do with me

Oh, how much I did cry
Believing an Ither person
Would find friendship with me

Yet this hope inside completely died
Upon the moment our eyes
Locked - and deception was detected

I loved her, I trusted her!
Yet I saw that projectors project
They've got shadows to protect

I saw that it's all a part of the game
No spiritualist can escape ego desires
Of money, sex, power, and fame

If they decide to play in the game

I wrote this prose for you
To keep out your eye
On vampires ready to suck you dry

Authenticity isn't something that can be bought
It is something earned
Wrought

Years it takes to get to know someone
It's a treasure
To be savored

Discernment is key
To exist in human society

The Ithers contain many illusions
Make sure, you come to your own conclusions
Before handing your

Power
Trust
And money

To someone so willing to "help you"
Out of their own necessity
To be seen too

Why Do I Strive for Fallacy

Why do I strive for fallacy?
Like it'll bring me some sort of satisfaction
My place in history?

I know I'm collecting
Moments, memories true to me

To add to the encyclopedia
Of humanity, for the galaxy
Record keepers of every living memory

Until we decide
We'd rather let certain memories die
Which we ask and wishes are granted

Why do I strive for fallacy?
When the golden egg is me?

Who I am at my core
Without labels or categories
Multidimensional, having many hues

That are all allowed
Accepted, treasured

Being quantum isn't fallacious
It is delicious
And not everyone can see

A multidimensional crystal
Only we can witness that of ourselves
No fallacy could ever reveal such beauty

Yet excruciating it is to continually
Share, put myself out there

And receive nothing in return

SWEEPING

Idly holding onto a broom
Longing,
Looking through,
The walls of the room

A longing, gazing into the past
Back in time of moments
Gone much too fast

Memories of sweet romance
Or perhaps
Wandering dreamily into the future

These moments to pass
A kind of torture

Could it be, another option?
A stare, a vision of caution

Eventually statue stature breaks off
Cleaning commences
Letting off a slight scoff

A SHIFT

How can I move from

To

Trying to help people
Who are stuck in pain
The shadows of society

Allowing myself to be
Allowing people to find me
No longer trying to rescue others

Always wanting to help someone
They know how to receive
From themselves or the Universe
They don't want help

By being myself
Others feel inspired
Wanting to connect, to grow
Evolve, become better
Not for anyone but themselves

Always speaking to them
Hoping they'd listen to save
Their own lives
Like that of my dad dying
Fighting & defending with him
Hoping that he'd see
The sunshine paradigm
Available here?

People wanting
To learn about gardening
And growing their own food
Gardening healthy thoughts
Inside their brain room

This for me is a challenge
I see so much adversity
I feel like I can assist

Helpless I am, drowning
In everyone else's misery

Sacrificing myself
To hopefully help another
In a pool of decaying insanity

I won't go down with the ship
So what'll it take?

I sink myself deeper
And deeper, and deeper
Into the throes of nature
Because nature is real
And *does* listen.

To-Do List Item

I'm just another item on your to-do list
Rushing to check me off
Only to forget about me for another year

It's clear.

You don't have to say anything

Dog, Ma!

Ma! Your dog is out of control!
It runs around
Barking incessantly
Sticking its nose
Into people's buttholes

Ma, put your dog on a leash
Reel in those beliefs
Teach that dog of yours
To heel

Let others enjoy their lives
Without dogs sprinting up to them
Casting fear into their eyes

DESPISING THE "LIGHT"

I'm trying to decide why I despise
The spiritual community and their goals for unity

I'm trying to decide why I
Became so bitter inside after

Following guides online
"Who's intentions were best for me"

I'm trying to decide why I
feel so wronged by a minister

Whose sinister ways of exorcism
Affected me so that years later I'm still feeling cold

I'm trying to decide
Why I

Stopped believing in magic
Was it tragic?

That I believed in something so much
And it failed me, when I needed it the most

I lay bitter, cold
Melting around me, the snow

Did I sell my soul?
Pursuing a career path my higher self told

Me to pursue, in joy, and joyful it is at times
Cultish behavior puts me behind

Rigidity, sharp points
Fitting into authority's rusty joints

That perhaps I'll be able to make it somewhere
If I stopped to care about me and my needs

Yet I move at the pace of society's machine
Hoping financially the Universe will provide for me.

What happened to the work last year
Finding divinity within myself

In rest
And release of fear?

Soft, Mercury gliding waters
Being mother god's daughter

Ebbing and flowing with the tides?
Ugh, that way makes me want to hide!

How is it possible to be a velvety flower
In a harsh world hungry for power?

I am gentle at best but my place remain unclear
How can I function here without fear

Fully supported
And not shed a tear?

FAME SHAME

Desiring fame has me feeling

Shame.

I know better than this
Yet I act amiss

I say I want to be seen
Yet my ego wants to be a celebrity
Getting paid to be me
I don't actually have to do anything
If I'm famous

Desiring fame
Is a total illusion
I could never contain what it
Takes to have celebrity status
Nor do I even want that

The ego desires fame
Confuses it with
The desire
To be noticed
For my pain
And for my pleasures
The things that keep me sane

Why, dear one
Do you not share your talents?
Always looking for controversy
To put your voice into more misery

Why, dear one,
Do you forget your talents?
Your light?
The things that make you bright?
That silly music you write so dear
Makes you happy, isn't it clear?
Why not spend your time

Perfecting your tunes to shine?
Or create more art
To show your experiences on Earth?

Controversy
Arguing
Conflict
Misery
Are all things we "have answers to"
Please listen to me!
I've been through it too!

So much noise in the world
Because of vices
Minds forever twirled

Out of the mind
Resides
Paradise
Beauty

We don't need the vice

Augmented

Starry crown molding
What's unfolding
Prickly hair
Melancholy
Shadows cover the keyboard

Tension up the spine
Why why why
Can't I do this right
You play my favorite chord
It sounds better when you play it
I'm a lousy musician who's never made it

ASH TRAY

I can't believe the way
You teased me
Tortured me
But I thought it was normal
To roll my eyes and leave things unsaid

I can't believe you'd call me ash tray
Sure, my name is Ash
Ha ha
But you said it almost everyday
And laughed in that way
You'd flick your tongue out
Like you were mocking me
Like saying "fuck you"
As the microspit flung into the air
Like you were jealous or something
All with a sarcastic smile sewn to your face

Why did you have to call me ash tray?
You didn't even smoke

To Let Something Die

Surely
To live peacefully
Everything must be seen
In neutrality
Because everything exists
As long as thoughts persist

Don't you know
That in order to grow
We must leave old things behind
By starving them
Casting them out of the mind

Activists
Pacifists
Cynicists
Criticists
Expertcists
"Surely know what they're talking about"
Yet all the things they fight for
Or against
Keep the thing they dislike
Alive

If you want something to die
Let it die
Quit giving your attention to it
Just let it die!

When the last person leaves it behind
It will disappear
Dissipate into the atmosphere
And we will be free of it

Ashley Lynn

Thank God You're Dead

This feeling in my chest
Puts me at unrest
Pacing,
Racing
Not my heart
But anxiety

I can't live with or without you
Without feeling a hole there
Too much you did care
Smothering me out
Of my mind's
Own thoughts

Trained me, you did
To feel, be, think like you
I'm not sure where
I begin
And you end

I'm grateful everyday that you're dead
I wouldn't be able to handle it
Yet in your wake
I mistake
Your old paradigm
For mine

Emotional Musical

Our feelings
Can take us on journeys
Quite elaborate, mind you
Sometimes they need to be acted out
A dramatic period piece
To understand their truth

Victim Mindset

I have to get myself out of this mindset
I have to
It's skewing my sense of reality
Serving
Others and their opinions
Desires
Changing who I am so I'm not like them
Or not like what they don't like
It's confusing
Who am I actually?

No, I can't save the world
My mission? No longer serving the world
No matter of "influencing"
"Inspiring"
"Aspiring"
Can make me succeed

Be the change you wish to see?
In this world of misery
I feel like I'm floating on top
Of a pool of complete muck
Being a lotus flower perhaps
Pure of heart
Without a chance
A lotus flower can't change
The muck it grows in below

All I can do is be a lotus flower
I can't do anything else anymore
I've forgotten my pure heart
Tainted by the words of the world
That appears to be so fucked
But it's what we watch,
That makes us think that

Ashley Lynn

I'm tired of writing against society
Thinking of ways to help this planet
It's a blip in our evolution
Our attitudes and perspectives make us feel bad

But we're not

We're figuring things out

I'm sick of hearing
That service to self is bad
Just because I serve myself
And keep myself healthy
Happy
Joyful
In my own unique way

Sharing what does make me happy
Doesn't make me a bad person
It makes me sane
Serving is insanity

Move Forward

There's no way but forward
      no matter how long I decide to stay stuck

There's no way but forward
      even if my mind feels like muck

There's no way but forward
      failing time and time again

Spring always comes around
      even when I don't have a plan

The sun continues to shine
      when my dreams sleep, not alive

I must move on now
      maybe they'll awaken somehow

Or perhaps I'm meant to sow new seeds
      and let go of the old dreams

To redefine myself anew
      with new friends to join me too

Ashley Lynn

THIS EVER PERVADING FEELING

What is the meaning
Of this ever pervading feeling
That there's so much more
To experiencing?

Surely, there's more than practicality
This invisible reality
I am in, quiet
Moments as these

All I want is to
Float in this realm
Forget the rest,
It's making me drown

I know that's why I'm here
When I think the answer is clear
I end up in this ever pervading feeling
Daydreaming, grasping for meaning

Bring You Up

Don't let it bring you down
Invite what brings you up

Our minds
Create   reality
Our   feelings
Make   actuality
Society
Can train   you to
Fit into   a mold
To do what you're told

It can get you down
Emotions, programs
Thoughts, paradigms

A universal law states
That our mind,   thoughts create
For "good"   or   for "bad"
It's all relative
To values you have

Instead of saying
"Don't let it get you down,"
Why not say
"I allow that which'll bring me up,"
A play on words, sure
Yet the Universe has no terms
It'll bring you what you ask for

Don't let it get you down
Attract situations
Renditions
That'll make you say such a thing
Inviting in scenarios
To reaffirm such beliefs

"I allow that which'll bring me up"
Is a sure phrase that'll invite a full cup

What is Life?

Lay.
Ponder.
Is life a wonder?
A place of beauty unseen?
Or is existing a tragedy?

A purpose for it.
Yes.
Finding purpose is a quest.

One may search an entire lifetime for an answer

Once revealed, only life's over

Searching
Wondering
What is the point of all this?

Sure, there's opportunities to experience
Love and bliss

It's true we can make Earth a better place

But what about when I'm laying here
Feeling like a disgrace?

Hope is always found, true

The tragedy lies within, on those days feeling blue
For me, far from few

I'll keep waking up,
Living day by day

I'll seek purpose in the moment,
Whatever it may

DOGMA

Everyone must
If within you trust
Do things often
That break open dogma

That thing you're so against!!
Why not give it a rest?
And do it once
Compassion you'll entrust

For it's dogma that keeps us separate
Hateful
Spiteful
"Oh how could you!"

But wrong in one's eyes
Is right in another's
And to truly honor all life
No one must suffer

DECEMBER AT THE HOLLOW

Walking fast pace
With no ice skates
Holes torn through icy skin

Bubbles arise
The shadows, they cry
Deep beneath a murky surface

Bare feet loose on an earth dam
Damn,
Boxed up all these years

Needles above
Catch the shouts beneath
Filtering the air

For her, they came
The only reliable

Leap of faith, inside a thrill
Outside, faking apathy
Why do I bottle up to appear tough?

Bare feet on icy ground
The only thing that brings me alive
The only thing I can feel

A thrill

Electricity in water

ℱERTILIZER

To be honest, life is hard right now
I don't want to complain, I have so much to be grateful for
Life continually ebbs and flows between great moments
And terrifying moments
I'm feeling relieved overcoming some of my deepest fears
And daunted facing the bigger ones

There is no certainty of what the journey is
But there's certainty in the outcome that will happen
There's no way we can fail
There's no way it's not happening
There's certainty in every synchronicity that affirms the path today
But that's it for now
No preview of the future

I think I'm most scared of the journey
Because there's so much to face
It's like swimming in adversity
The "how" has become a hopeless question
The "how" will come by way of magic
There's no logic to these things
None whatsoever
The Universe is quantum
Nothing's a straight line anymore

I'm finding out that the only way through is forward
I'm finding out that plans change everyday
I'm finding out that my old dreams weren't a disaster
They were stepping stones for where I am today
And I'll have to use those skills and ideals
Once again
Because paradigm shifters are oft
Forced to take the path less traveled

So even if it seems like I'm starting over
I'm not
Because lessons learned in years prior
Are fertilizer for the seeds sown today

Sad Poems

I don't like writing sad poems
I love to share my light
Happiness, nobody cares about
Attention snapped to the plight

It makes me sad
Knowing I only get attention
When I'm crying
In trauma
Having problems
Lost

But if I have a celebration day
Joy, great play!

Nobody wants to hear it.

People Pleasing Rebel

I do everything to be a good person
That I want to be bad
Pleasing everyone
Leaves me sad

ꞁOVE TOO SOON?

We bonded strongly
"I love you," was the first sentence
You typed to me

You told me you loved me
Before I even had the chance to see
Who "you" were

Months later lost in chatter
Mine? Or yours?
I think the latter

I've created my best life, progress is slow
I observe you in your beginningness
Stifled to grow

So much of me, I see in you

I'm no longer that person…
Keeping you around
Makes me spiral round and round

Why do we overthink?
Let it go, it's not worth
The scientific analysis

Life's meant to be simple
I know this, my deepest truth
A simple life is a good life

I have all I need
It keeps getting better and fuller

In our mind wanderings
We falter, getting lost in a desert
Each grain of sand a thought

Creating a land of desolateness
Forever, you and I
Alone

Trickery the mind had me following
Mirrored in you and your being
My body, unrest feeling

I don't need to go deep
To share my past
To have friendships that last

The key
Once again, is
Simplicity

Going deep is saying nothing
Exchanging a glance
Says a thousand words

GUITAR WITH NEW FRIENDS

So much is said
Without saying a word
The phenomenon like purple haze
Hanging in a wood box these days

Speaking through sounds
Plucked on metal strings

Weaving in and out
Of the mist inside
Battered emotions unwind

We're always so alone

I try to intuit what's going on
Listening deeply into the song
Or testing trust between new friends
Will it last, or will it end?

GUARDED

I've waited my whole life for these moments
Held onto a dream that had no hope
Continued on trying
Alone in a room full of mirrors
Not knowing they were two-ways

Exposed, I hide
I couldn't believe he died

Now I'm here
I feel more clear
My ability to share
Dampened down
Hardly there

Scared of shining my light
So many times
Criticized
Teased
Relentlessly tried to please
Always laughing at myself
As they did to me
The jester joker, I was to them
No one took me seriously
Except for he

You feel like family
My heart an open cave
You can only come in
If you can behave
Nobody is hurting me anymore

Energy I carry
Strumming notes on a fretboard
Create harmonies with other fretboards
Sounds for a coming age

Could this ever be something?

RELATIONSHIP PRISON

Relationships can be like a prison
Intricate indecencies with one another
Intimate most of the time
Until a fire ignites

At anytime, a catastrophe can happen
Sudden eruption may or may not
Have to do with you
Red, they reside inside

These moments, patterns reaming
The prison cell, caged in with
Their devil as they revel with the
Demons of their multidimensionality

The way out is through
Either unconditionality, merge you
Or an escape route
Be thought through

There's two ways
To leave jail
Wait, get out on bail
Or escape on a new trail

Love everyone, in moderation! I say
Unconditionality, momentarily
Can go a long way

Under-involvement
Gives them time to solve it
Their problems their own to fix

Ashley Lynn

SORRY FOR THE FAKERY

I'm fake to you // my feelings?
You shouldn't know they're true

Ghosting people // Seeing my bad habits in them
I don't want to experience them again

Honesty evaporates // I have so much to say about you
It wouldn't do you any good if you knew the truth

I love you, I really do!
But your life choices?
Boy, what are you to do?

You are stupid // Incapable
Too sensitive // Ridiculous

Even though I struggle too // With the same things as you

Armor on, defenses up // I need to be stronger than you
I need to show myself // I can do what you can't do

A boundary goes up // Just shut up!
Grow some balls // Do the hard things

I can't listen to your mind flings

These things I say to myself
Even though slowly I'm building wealth
I make excuses why my progress isn't showing
Time will tell, not any of my doing

Sometimes // A break is what's best

Let the relationship rest // Time is always the test
To see if it's truly meant to be // If we're meant to last

SHUN

I find that I can't // Help to race
To ghosting // Once things get weird

Disappear // Shun you!
Why do me wrong? // You'd never know
Maybe a whisper in the air // You'll hear
Of me reeling // About you dear

Years pass // Until I decide, at last
To forgive this person // I love them so
Then next thing I know // They're dead
Dust in the wind // They blow

Sometimes I shun people online
They slip up once // And that's it! I'm done!
They preach all day // Do the opposite of what they say
Misleading others, have you! // People will always follow a guru

Yet there's always a reason // For each personal season

The people in our lives

Are there for good reason

KINDRED SPIRIT

You can preach something
Or you can be something
The secret to doing it
Is doing it

It's simple to live simple

Getting to know you
Not by your past
But by the way you are and
What floats around your mind

Desires in a chamber

Brown and beige rubber boots
Folded down
Down to the ankles
Both pairs crossed

Bring a sense of home to me

Other earth wanderers like me
Souls unbound
Limits unwound
Ready to soar

Experience well worn

ᛁTHER SWIM

What's the point of all this madness?
The more we have, the more sadness
Is there an end to comparison and contraction?
We as souls desire expansion

Who's a voice in a vast ocean?
If no one can see me, in all this motion
Surely drops are minuscule in *that* water
A hive mind mentality, all drowning

Off the ithers I feel myself content,
Amongst simple, like minded folk
Whose presence doesn't make me choke

In tiny towns across this land
I see before me, laid out a plan
A whisper reveals a new blueprint for life
One created to end my strife

I feel it awakening in me, living
In harmony with REAL community
Talking and communing with trees
Writing poetry, music to sing

Unleashing my true destiny

My place is not within the ocean
Spreading re-runs on the 'net
It is here in this physical life I live
A life without the debt

The biggest impacts we can make
If it's humanity we want to wake
Are to be with each other in physicality
Talk to our neighbors about new realities

Pursue truth by going within
There's no need to internet swim

Programming

Who are you
Outside of programming?

A wake up
Suddenly realizing
The awareness of being aware
A feeling that you're actually here
That everything you learned in life
May... potentially be a lie
Everything you learned in life
Was training
To conveyor belt
On a cog
In the machine

Quickly! You decide!
I must myself, redefine!
Seeking, searching
For anything
Anything
That is not "that"

Some speaker, perhaps
Catches my glance
A chance
To hear it from someone
Who's escaped the trap

Yet

Let's not replace old programming
With new
By becoming like someone
Embodying their hue

BEFRIENDING SHADOWS

‖ Acceptance ‖

\\ I can make friends with my darkness, accept my past and
the world around me, shedding skins at last //

ADVERSITY UNCONDITIONALLY LOVES

When adversity
         unconditionally
                  loves me
It's like the war is over
On the battlefield, completely stopped
                  Looking around at each other
                           Wondering
                                    Why were we fighting in the first place?

Yeah I'm still ready to fight
Still ready to defend, hanging onto my tight rope
I feel that any slip up in the adversity
Myself, I need to protect

When adversity
         unconditionally
                  loves me,
I find myself under a canopy of trees
         wondering
What was I so afraid of all this time?

Indeed,
I find it challenging
         to coexist with adversity
                  with polarity.
Such differences in the way we see society
         the way we go on living
                  we are thriving in our differences yet
         could we ever come together?
Could we ever work together?
I'd say yes, but,
                  love everyone in moderation.

You love me unconditionally,
         but do I love you unconditionally?
I find my personality reeling
         thoughts peeling
                  inside my mind

Yes, we are both benign.
We are both benevolent.
We can both see souls clearly
We both intend for the best in any situation
                    we wish the best for each other.
But,
        the way we see things is so different.

Sometimes I can think that you're blind
        but no
                our paradigms
        are different in this world.

We are together.   Yet separate.

        This is one of the greatest tests of allowing things to be.

        Of course,
                there's no way
                        either of us are changing
                                the world with our thoughts
                                        with our beliefs
                                                we create our own world
                                        we create what works best for each of us,
                                and we must
                        exist
        in our own paradigms
                overlapping energies
                        often could feel like a war zone
                                but
                        keeping distance
                keeps the peace
        and that's the piece
I wish to leave

How does it feel to be unconditionally loved by adversity?
        It's very strange to me
                I'm left without words
                        I am speechless.

I don't know how to go on from here
    for once my channel is clear
        for once I am able to be a seer
            for once I can open up my voice box
      and let out all that's inside of me
    because adversity
        unconditionally loves me,
            and no matter what I say or do
                they will love me like any mother would do

The key
I'm starting to see
Is to focus on relatability
    Yes, we have this diversity
        That can be bone chilling
    Yet
We have commonalities
Things that make us sing!
Laugh, jeer, come together
    This is what we can focus on

And the best way
To handle adversity
Is to let it be
Let the diversity be
It is okay to disagree
Let's not focus on that
Let's focus on unity

I Need You

I can't hate everyone
No matter how hypocritical they are
Or contradicting, or being an obnoxious projectile

We are all trying to be our best
Trying to be Perfect
We never will be, we're not supposed to be
So let's forgive each other

Perceptions of you could be truth
Or some subconscious tale
We can try to be friends
Chances are we'll get along
If we allow each other
To sing our unique songs

So quick to wrong or right
Yet duality exists
In the minds of humans
All we can do is train our nervous system
Something new

All I'm trying to say
Is that I forgive you, it's okay
I'm sorry I held that grudge
And stagnated our relationship to sludge
It hurt me more than you, I still value you
And the qualities beau that make you true

I forgive you because... I need you
You are a mirror to me of something inside
That makes me happy

I'm sorry I fragmented
And thought bad things of you
Family you are
Sharing this forgetful scar
Unity is better than purgatory

HIBERNATION

Restless creatures
Sleep infinitely
Awaiting the days of warm weather
Anxiously ready to tear

HOLLOW

My heart is hollow
Like like the arches in Utah
Brisk weather in winter
Eroding away the edges
The hole a wind tunnel

Hollow

Never See Myself

One day, I realized
I'd never get to see myself
With my own two eyes

Saddened, I became
For how could I see
What it's like to be me?

A soul, the spirit
Has no body, no form
Yet here I am inside of one
I can't see her, torn

My head spins
Am I doing wrong, right?
Inside I can't see me
Personal perception out of sight

A light, she guides
"Why not step out for awhile?
Cast an outward gaze upon you
Notice her smile"

Instantly uplifted
The clouds have drifted
And now I can see her beauty

Beauty is not a physical thing
It's the passion in the eye
For doing something
Lovingly

Being beautiful is something you dare
Letting go of the physical to truly be there

TRUE BEAUTY

Sometimes I struggle to see my own beauty
Even though I feel beauty
In my surroundings

Sometimes I look in the mirror and get nervous
Seeing a young girl
In the presence of such a huge soul

On my human face I see blemishes
Miniature volcanoes
Gigantic glasses
How could this tiny person
Be good enough for the soul within?

I close my eyes and go to a safe place
A place inside of love and grace
Where souls roam in gardens everlasting
Angels heal and protect
Divine light blasting

The way to break the nervousness
Is to speak to myself loving kindness
As I speak
The goddess is unleashed
And slowly, over time
The heaviness is eased

I'm reminded that the beauty I notice
When glancing around the forest
Reflects the beauty of me

Just as the flower
Radiates angelic power
I too am that graceful force

The angels say, "Can you see the
Expression on your face,
When you admire a tranquil place?

See yourself from the flower's point of view
They see green eyes glowing too

The relaxation, appreciation
Of the muscles in your face
The grace from you emanates
Brilliant beauty, it creates
All from being, love
Splendor in the soul

Your gaze, it softens
Becoming oneness
A part of peace and paradise
This dear one, is beauty"

The next time I gaze in the mirror
I can see myself, a flower so dear
I am a human, I bloom
From a seed of a star
On the other side of the moon

LEAVE THAT ONE THING BEHIND

You have the

Ability
Power
Creativity
Insight
Love

Inside of you to thrive

Joyfully
Peacefully
Gracefully
Abundantly
Lovingly

And to live your best life

There's one thing
You must leave
Behind

The battle within

There's no need to
Fight anymore

Dear one

Miss the Sun

My blazing star in the sky
You're a million miles away
I sway
Missing your warm touch

It's hard to be here
Not there
Where the air
Is easier to breathe

Existing on two feet
Magnetized to this planet
Gets to me sometimes

I confess, I can have fun here
When I let go of seriousness

Make this easier for me
Pretty, pretty please?

\\ She replies with the whisper of a salty breeze

Golden molecules dancing on fire painted rocks //

TEARS OF BELONGING

Overwhelmed, over tired
I can't conspire the
Hot tears rolling down my face

I don't want you to see
The way I'm feeling
I don't want to be known as
A crier
For desire
To earn your love

I weep, I cry
With tears in my eyes
Of all the years gone by
Alone, without a tribe

That here and now
I stand grateful
With my sisters by my side

The laughter, the love
Eye gazing and rounds of hugs
For once I feel belonging
Instead of longing
Longing
Longing
For this day to come

Sisters, if you catch my tear
Know it's only because
You're here
And I need not fear

Another Human

To be cared for by another human
Is better than anything on a screen
To be cared for by another human
Means you're truly seen

Hugs and kisses on the daily
Eyes locked in, together gazing
Connecting
Dreaming
Sleeping
Gleaming

Preparing energy for each other
Keeping us alive, unlike any other
Sometimes we sit on the couch, silent
Others are loud, dancing on the carpet

Through the seasons we trail on
Each one different,
Even if I'm having a summery winter
You could be living winter winter
We come together and on the bed slither

Isn't the point of being physical
To experience physicality?
Five senses reality?
Experimenting
With all that we can be?

So why is it?
We spend our time on screens?
Or even creating things for watching?
When we have the freedom
To embody anything we'd like to be?

Here and Now

ENERGY MOVING

It's inspiring, perhaps?
To feel melancholically pensive
Being indecisive
Yet there's a way to move everything

Some people write poetry when they're melancholy
Some people make movies when they're happy
Some people cruise down mountains when they're sad
Being in nature can make an anxious person glad
Some people write intricate novels to explain themselves
Some people manically clean when feeling overwhelmed
Some people travel when their soul magnetizes for them
Being in water transforms dullness to enchantment

There's a way to alchemize anything
And you know what?
No way is good or bad
It just is

Because art is not a noun
It is a verb

It's up to you to move the energy

Ashley Lynn

THE BEST WAY TO HELP EARTH

You're one person
You're small
I beg you

Don't put the world's problems on your shoulders

The best way to help
In dire situations
Possible occurrences
Is to set aside worry
And focus on positive possibilities
Think about what you *want*,
For you and everyone else

If you catch yourself worrying,
Conspiring,
Spiraling,
Take a deep breath
Call forth your power
And intent for the highest outcome

Believe that you and everyone else
Is on a positive path
We're all okay
Relax
Let go

Focus on soulful fulfillment
And allow the collective thought
Form of greater possibilities
To manifest before our eyes

EDIBLES

Smoking before work
Sneaking around
With an edible in my front overall pocket
Zipped
No one can see when I slip
Away
No one notices
Because I'm invisible anyway

This shadow of mine
The fear of being caught
Red handed!
You stoner!
Live forever in a dungeon pit
Of my shame for you!

No longer exists.

Partially because
I am invisible
I am sneaky
Sly, fox

I'm an adult now
Just because I smoke
Weed doesn't mean
I can't be a functioning
Member of society

What it actually shows
Is the empowerment
That goes
With being able to
Indulge in pleasures
In things that awaken my heart treasures
And be "normal" anyway
Without dealing with your shame

Ashley Lynn

SOMETIMES WE GOTTA DIE

To shine from the inside, old parts of us must die
Find out who we are on the other side

People change, yeah they change
We all come from a different range

We must shed, shed our leathery skins
Of who we were, when we begin again

It is hard to let go, move with the flow
You've got better places to go

Promise, you will reach such a bliss
You don't want to miss

Death sounds bleak, a gentle part of nature
There's nothing scary about dying

Think about the mycelium
They're alive, thriving, feasting on death

A mushroom dies, eaten by fungi
To become part of the soil, part of the web of life

Is death a bad thing?
Something we should be loathing?

Once old parts of us die
We empty out, barren, we lie

Potential grows into new self, a rose!
Feasting on the old

We shed to the ground
Once dead

MULLING

Ruminating

Has been my problem
All along
Mulling cider for a decade
Making my defenses strong

I forgot to tell myself
Let go, move on

I'll live

We all have hard times

My pain isn't unique

To continuously think
About my problems and the bad stuff
Ferments cider to vinegar
Forever a heart bitter

I'll live

It's time to move on

A MYSTERY WITHIN

I can feel Her within, a mystery She is
The encyclopedia of emotions

Feelings are fleeting in the moment
Emotions become characters themselves

The mystery of She, all of these

Anger   Rage
         Grief   Longing
   Bliss   Ecstasy
        Wild   Contentment
Peace   Joy   Grace   Love
   Terror   Disdain   Pain

All worthy of being without vain

She who is free can be
Everything unapologetically

She is not too much, too little, she just is
She lets herself run wild, inside, a free child

Sure, it can be helpful to serve others
But what about thyself?
We live in temple bodies, infinitely full of wealth

The key to being free is to balance emotions
Allow them expressed fully, in each moment, surely

A prairie
An ocean
A whirlwind
A waterfall
A stoic rock wall
A torrential rainstorm
A trickling stream

Entirety is serene

EMBODYING PARADOX

How could a spiritualist
One who wants harmony
Unity, expect that
If they can't mingle
With the masses?

Dare I hold this awareness of myself
Go out in the world
And experience true wealth

Hide not behind screens
In isolated forests
But mingle with the masses
To understand their angsts

So I go, fishy sun, I am
Able to embody all the zodiac
Mingle I can in any pool in front of me
As long as it possesses no evil
I will not attract entities

One day I find myself picking
Tomatoes at a greenhouse farm
Chops licking, mingling with farmers
Growing food is important
To keep a body of light

The next thing I know
I'm zooming fast on the go
Yellow feet with pink toes
Roller ramps, here I go
A culture of angst
Of punk, eclectic tastes
Colored hair and ripped pants
Baggy shirts, fishnets
Music "distorted" - I digress
Emotions expressed in their finest
To relieve adversity and stress

Ashley Lynn

Smoothly warping, wefting
High priestess, a princess
Divine feminine essence
One that wears a dress
Femininity expressed, receptive, sacred
This part of me is personal
Standing on ethereal stumps
Watching the butterflies
Encircle me with light

Teleport me to rocks of iron ore
Red cathedrals soar into an oven sky
Baked the ocean right out of the desert!
Vortexes, most high
Spiritualists reside here, metaphysicians
Understanding the core essence
Of energy, what bliss

Energy is fluid - neutral, its finest
The way to use it is intent
Nothing is good or bad
Until perception is put upon it

Lower some notches - I'm drinking hops
Mingling with commoners the way they've
Done for years
All have a mellow undertone of a day well sown
Laborious, their lives are, an illusion, the toil

Spiritualists fail to see...
That the whole purpose of being
Is to experience all the facets of humanity
To integrate them all, to mingle
Any rejection of one is a rejection of self
No matter of praying or Source protecting
Can erase the facets in everyone's face

JAGGED WOOD

I let myself get lost
    In a metaphorical world
        Of spiny trees and jagged rocks

I thought it would bring me answers
    Salvation
        To know the truth
            About our civilization

So much I learned
    The potential history
        Of humanity
            My, what a story!
                Evolving
                    From a star system so far
                And moving from here to there
            Until eventually we got here
        With the help of others of course

    This reality was like the hazy sun
        Above a sheet of wildfire smoke
            From thousands of miles away
                Seeing that I am affected by
            People's actions
        From light years
    And timely years
Away

Darkness abided when
    I stepped further in
        Learning of conspiracies
        That maybe beings
            Make the human species
                Trapped
                Slaves
                Feeding an invisible race
            And bowing down
        To culture icons
    And corporate gods

Truth is flexible, I found

I can observe all the thorny trees
      Trees without arrays of leaves
            Understand them
            Dissect them even
      Yet, are thorny trees truth?

They're a facet,
      But not all of it

It was only when I walked out of the jagged wood
      That I saw myself standing there
            Again
            She stood there when I entered
      When I remained
      And when I exited

She is always there with me
      Guiding
            Showing me
            The polarity
      Or perhaps the entirety
      Of universality
Everything exists
And can be free

I found
      That I can explore anything
            I wish and please
      Jagged forests
Or waterfalls of iridescence
      It is all a choice
            I can choose at anytime

Because I am always free

My Music

Today I accepted the fact that
I'll never be a professional musician

I lack the precision, emotion, skill, dedication
To do such a thing everyday

Could I ever move a person
With my silly, quirky tunes?

My personality forever a child
Feeling everything magically

Not seriously
My music, smiley fun

Who would seriously listen to my music
Amateur-ly written, all fun in the moment

Nothing to master, more like a tune
From the Budapest Room

Surely I could write a musical
With all my nature rambling tunes

A catastrophe, my 20's
Almost finished with nothing to show

I never want to change
The way I am, so strange

My music makes me happy
Even if it makes me estranged

I want not to be loved by children
They are the easiest to vibe with

But adult kids to see me in them
Do they love me because they feel my sadness?

Ashley Lynn

I'll never be a professional musician
The doubt that always creeps in

All the times I poured my soul out
Creating unconditionally, courageously

For no one to hear me

Once again it's too painful
To carry the dream

I'm sorry, I want to do this
Maybe it will happen

Even if it takes my lifetime

REALIZATION OF ME

I sit in this leather seated car
Something much nicer than
I'm used to, clean
The roof an entire window!
For clear seeing
Of the stars in the sky

I sit in the backseat
Like I did as a child, wondering
As I look out the window
At the forests passing by
In the blink of an eye - My,
How many ticks are in those
Forests anyway? After picking
About sixteen off the dogs last night

My burlap cardigan hangs heavy off my skinny body
The bright flower socks resting
I have no inhibitions
I turned into this free spirit
Who is floating
On a giant rock in space
Knowing that working too hard
Or becoming a slave to the human race
Wouldn't do me any good
Does that make me a disgrace?

Maybe everyone could use a little more free time
Some space to let their minds unwind
They too can release their inhibitions
Feel how amazing it is to be a spirit
In this cool fleshy body
And feel how the trees love us so
The nature spirits blessing our toes
As we walk on their sacred land
They care for intricately
So we can cohabitate Earth in harmony

But I digress, my purple backpack
Being through a mess
An oversized purse filled with a planner I don't use
A poetry book filled with mind scribbles
As if my phone notes weren't enough

And that sketchbook that I want to draw in
But never do
It is like that thorn in my side
Bugging me that I don't do it
That fancy pencil I found at a health talk
Underneath archaic theater seats in a crumbling church auditorium

My purse is surprisingly with me too
Filled to the brim with more journals
And of course a wallet
With many ways to pay for things
Without going into debt

And all the homeopathic goodies
The rose roll on oil
The elderberry stress mints
Headphones
And those two black licorice I stashed away
So he and I could have a surprise one of these days

One pocket full of poop bags
For unpredictable chihuahua shits
In the middle of the road

It's not surprising
The glasses case with sunglasses I'd never wear
Because I prefer the UV rays blasting in my eyes
Making me cosmically awake

The shoes I spent more than I ever had before
Because they promise better posture by feeling barefoot
More room for my toes to move and be free
It's all about being more free

Cargo pants with ten pockets
Is surely more freeing than jeans clenching my crotch
And graphic tees for days
I'm sure as hell not wearing a bra anymore
And since I don't shower much
My hair goes into braids of the Dutch
And under a hat with petroglyphs on it
My soul home, of course

Shall we go back to my backpack?
I spent way more than necessary
But it has a lifetime warranty
I could get a new one for free if this one breaks
But five years in? Hardly looks used
Despite being abused and taken on airplanes
Trains. Car rides. Hikes. Libraries. Coffee houses
Osprey, like my spirit animal, bird of prey
Not that I'm preying on anyone
Just embodying the eye of her
And floating with the wind
Spotting the auspicious
Time for catching opportunities

Inside will always reside my laptop
And various accessories for her
Like a technology fashionista
I couldn't live without these things
Creating beauty with my camera,
Headphones, various cords & cards

The front pocket always contains
A packet of napkins
At least a few years old
Just in case I need to blow my nose!

The blue water bottle
Clearly out of date
What, like seven years ago?
My, it is so much better to use things until they are gone
Because it is too much to think about how to recycle seeming waste

Interesting it is
To break out of cosmic thoughts
The mind
And to witness who I am here and now
And I love me
I'm so funny
In all my quirks and such

It makes life so much simpler
When I don't have to think about my physicality so much
My mind is where it's at
So vast and open like the desert

Red rocks glowing

Not because they're red

But because they're alive

RECEIVED

I give
Unconditionally
Knowing
I'll never receive that which I give to them
Back

Regardless I frolic
In the bliss of my love
Knowing
That which I give to others
I give to myself

That is enough
To make manifest
My dreams and desires
To self acknowledge
To love self unconditionally
So much
That I can give so freely

And by that
I'm received

WILDLY UNRELIABLE

I'm wildly unreliable
A world where time stands still
Words pour through my mouth
Creativity, a thrill

Alive, yes, blood does not
Flow through my veins
But light, there's
No more room for pain

Pain is perception
Even in mass rejection
Pleasure is found
Listen for a certain sound

Myself, I cannot give away
Time is precious, I won't pay
For my regrets later in life
So I live feral without strife

I'm sorry,
I won't conform
To the lifestyles of society
Considered the norm

I'd rather be poor
Than sell my soul away
Freedom is nature
Nothing to pay

Ash

My name is Ash, not *ash tray*
But Ash, a soft substance
Powdery and pure, innocence
Nature's blistery way of starting fresh

Don't you know new life grows from ash?
Pure, raw, new life
The hope after tragedy
A new canvas for Earth to play

Ash

The perfect metaphor of my life
Constantly cycling
Erupting
Destroying
Purifying
Resting
Rising
Growing
Evolving
Creating

Ash is new beginnings
Ash, the ability to start fresh with an open mind

All those times you called me ash tray
Or jack ash - you tore me down

You convinced me my family
Was bad for me, but it was you
I was shining, lightning, you'd find some way
To steal my thunder, make me invisible

You burned me up, yet here I am
Thriving on the tragedy I left behind

Without you

Ashley Lynn

Ashley Lynn

Together, Out of the Woods

{{ Healing, Hope }}

\\ Emptying out and tilling the ground for a new self //

CREATE YOUR FATE

I started acting my own age
Instead of living in my old ways

"Don't lose your spirit child
You should be running wild
The call, it's all
In your heart, all the wild

Let's create together
Birds of a feather
And weather
A new age"

EARN IT

Fake it till you make it?

Why not change it to
Work it till you earn it?

When I feel I've earned it

That's where the true treasure lies

A New Society

I want to live in a new society
Where women are celebrated
For being mothers, home-caretakers
Volunteers, community leaders
Without the expectation to make
Money or do anything more

Being these is enough.

I want to live in a society
Where women can relax
Take time for themselves
Can be loved and pampered
Be supported financially
Without the shame

I want to live in a society
Where men can work less
Where they can feel safe and open
Where their emotions they can express
Without being ridiculed

I want to live in a society
Where gender roles rule not
Be whatever you are
And fill up your heart

I want to live in a society
Where people can love each other freely
Hug your neighbors on the street
See the best in each other
Without being sexually targeted
Without feeling shameful

I want to live in a society
Where people can follow their passions
Pursue creative obsessions
Whether or not it makes money
Where people aren't expected to work dead end jobs
That make them unhappy
Because working a job is socially acceptable

I want to live in a society
Where all "positions" are respected equally
Where we can all live peacefully
Without fighting for our limitations
Or the things we care about

I want to live in a society
Where people have abundance
It's a mindset you know
Open up the floodgates for all
Prosperity is a river to flow

Because life on this planet
Is meant to be pleasurable
All people rendered equal
Feelings so joyful
Along the normal human life qualms
So much of what we go through
Is because of these old social norms

Isn't it time now
For a storm
To shuffle
Alignment into place?

LIFE WITH DEMONS

I take my demons everywhere with me
There's no place they don't go
Over the hills and into the woods
On mountaintops covered in snow

My demons, my greatest companions
They ramble on with me
Nomadic adventures in nature's treasures
The road our home always somewhere new to go

We laugh and play in the sun all day
Kisses turn my face a'burn
Snaggletooth smiling, nothing conspiring

Together, we're safe here
There's nothing more to fear
A state of being, relaxed, healing

Oh, my demons, I love them so
More than anyone on Earth
They make my heart glow

Those demons, they're scared of everything
Gunshots, explosions, four-wheeled toys
New people, old people
Even innocent little boys

Threatened, always on the defensive
If they're triggered
Who knows what's a'happenin' next

What's that? Danger?!
Unleashed they become
A mind coated in glue
Oh no, what have I done?

Scrambling, I scrounge together
My demons, by the blue tether
Eyes enraged, ember-red

It's not their fault,
Their innocence is dead!
Someone hurt them
Before I could help them
Trust no one, inside they said

Forevermore my demons
Make sure no one can get closer
This pack they must protect
Any outsiders get left
In the dust

The only way they behave
Is temptation, enticing bait
Hold it out in front of them
Eyes follow, a pendulum

When they behave every once in awhile...
Give them a treat
Demons contained deserve a treat
Really, they do

Alas, I must reveal
My demons are my dogs
Manifested from within
My demons became real
For in reality? Not ideal!

If you approach me and I seem unfriendly
Know it's not you but my demons
On the leash, a disguise
Of my reeling mind

I Create For Me

I create for me
Although I put it on the ithers for everyone to see
At the core of it all
I create for me

I create for me
Capturing my favorite memories
Through screens
Is an act of love
For me

Going back to see
How I was in a moment
Seeing myself smile
Improving my skills
I do this all for me

If no one else sees
I'll admit, I feel uncertainty
Because everyone wants to be acknowledged
For the things that make them happy

SOVEREIGNTY IS KEY

Sovereignty, the catch phrase of our day, Sovereignty

It is realizing
Without conceptualizing
We have free will
In every situation
No matter what rendition
Is appearing to control us

What it is not...
Acting on others' thoughts
Oh, their views of reality
That's not for you to be

Nothing can control you
If you claim your sovereignty
You need not pay a spiritual seer
To activate that for thee

Anytime, one can declare
If they dare, shout it to the ethers!
Even the ithers...
Responsibility is there

Sovereignty
Is responsibility for yourself
A victim you're not anymore
Because victim hood
Is a choice
Trickery
Programmability

Once sovereignty is claimed
Paradise you can create
Heaven is on Earth, you see
This planet is best for us
We're born creators of reality

REQUIEM

May she
Rest in peace
A facet lost it
And returned back
To the beginning

She realized
Within her eyes
Her soul lies
Not fibbing, mind you
But resides

Her way
Or the Highway
The Highway indeed
For the Highway
Is consciousness's way
Her soul knows what's best for her
That clouded perceptions
Wishes
Couldn't dare
To show how much the spirit cares
To delay satisfaction
For a more fitting occasion
One of the highest timeline
That everyone may be sublime

The path to get "there"
Is almost never clear
To the Earthly seer
Who is unable to have a bird's eye
In the midst of a cry

No, dear one
Wait you must
Keep on your daily toil
For toil it is not
It is a way of life
To do things daily
With or without strife
But to move forward
Be insured
You will get "there"
When most aligned

She knows
Everyone is divine
No matter how difficult
They are divine
She is divine
She is safe here
She must care
Breathe the cold air

GRANDMOTHER WISDOM

Young one,
You're invisible
In the drip drops of ither ocean

Yet you're visible
In a physical world
A light to people you can see

Inspire the youth with alternatives
Plan and learn inquisitively
You are needed

In physicality instead of virtual reality
Because physicality
Is where you'll remain

PURSUE ENSUE

I will forever pursue the truth
The invisible, the potential
Of other people outside of humanity
Of the invisible forces in nature who
Communicate with me

But for now
I embrace my humility
Let go of insanity
And allow my existence to be
Meaningful

To me

MY GREATEST TRUTH

You can't rely on much these days
It seems
But one thing's true for sure
Nothing, *nothing,* is ever lost

This one phrase is something I can count on
Nothing can ever be lost,
It can only be found
It's always there
Available

All you have to do is ask

It is always somewhere

EXIST BLISS

Every glance
    I witness
        A still for a movie
            A divine photograph of beauty
                An intelligent-sound symphony
                Every moment in peace
            Like this is bliss
        And I know here, I'm home
    Falling in love
Rooted here from above

    It truly is my purpose here
        To bear witness, to lie still
            To exist, appreciate
                To be held in divinity
                    To express that creativity

Ashley Lynn

CONTENTING

At glance
A house on a hillside
Turned dusk
Whimsical nighttime

Stars twinkle yonder
Capturing you, to ponder

Before the eyes lies
An antique summertime
With the seasons, living
Nature forever giving

No reason for inventing
For contenting
Is already here

CHANGING CRAVINGS

My heart
Craves for changing
A reawakening
To who I am at my
Core

My mind wants to follow
Lost in the clouds
How to express in new ways?

A rabbit with new beginnings
The cicada
The butterfly
Embrace the change
It will all come naturally
With grace

TREEDOM

Tranquil tree in the park
The soul in me sees your spark
Ancient, the years passed
Through your rested bark
The many people you've watched
Through cycles of light and dark

Wise you are
A soul standing against time
I see your heart
As you see mine
Together, we talk
Through our minds

This tragedy will end
Once we unite

⁹NNER ᏟRITIC?

My inner critic might actually be my inner goddess

She is always bothering me, it seems
In another light, she encourages me, just be me

She makes me nervous, my reflection in the mirror
Inside I feel her, watching me with care

She loves me dearly
And knows it was hard
Coming here as a human
My remembrance of her in shards

Bits and pieces I remember
Times of a high priestess, a goddess of nature
Being this has been painful, living below my potential
Sometimes not of a choice, necessity of this reality

Still, she guides me if I'm able to listen
She has me follow my bliss, in light, I glisten

If bad thoughts arise in my mind
I get confused, is it her? // Or the trouble of being confined?
She'll come in strong // Tell me "that's wrong!"
Yet I confuse "that" for "you're" // An effect of a male lore

Slowly still, I recognize her voice
The more I silence the chaos by choice
I can hear her, I can truly hear her!
The grace in her eyes whispers in my ears

She's calling to me. I am set free
She's protective, you see, together we're one

As I move on I can open my heart
And sing my songs
Know I am love and nothing less
We can merge together and be our best

Ashley Lynn

Out of Water

Fresh
New
Steam pours out the shower
The gleam of my skin
Cleansed again

Out the window pane
The earth is bare
Raggedy, scrunched down
Wet, sloshy
Ripe with potential
Fertile
Like a freshly cleansed
Maiden
Ready to awaken

We are one of the same

TURNING TABLES

Oh, my love
How the tables have turned
Both of us battered, broken
Needing some tinkering
And here we are

Your confidence is outstanding
You've changed your vibe
Social setting, became stronger
No one can stop you
Not even me

It's not that it bothers me
That you've become successful
It bothers me that I haven't
And I put in the same amount of work

I'm disappointed in myself, I try to bring you down
Because it is painful to see you doing so well
Inside I'm dying a bit trying hard not to quit
To keep following my dreams
To be happy for yours manifesting
Before both our eyes

I feel like your shadow
I never wanted to wear the label
Wife
Because wives are the shadows of their husbands
They never seem to get any sort of acknowledgment
No matter how brilliant they are

I want to be successful and me
Not a shadow who piggy backs off your success

Something will surely change, it always does
You don't need to change, or dim your light
I want some help turning mine back on
Will you listen to my song?

TEACH HIM

'Tis true
Men haven't a clue of how
To love a woman, wild
'Tis true

Instead of shaming him, blaming
For the millennia of brutal
Rule, why not...teach him
How to love a wild woman true?

Innocence he is
My, he may not remember
Seven generations before
Couldn't have told him

Can you imagine being glorified
For dominating your wife?
Because your fathers,
Fathers
Fathers
Told you, these are the ways
And passed down
To the sons
Sons
Sons
Of mothers without voices
Their choices, in her DNA

How can he know
Another way?
Unless a woman of grace
With strong wits pithing her face
Dominates
Gently

To show him

EMPTYING OUT

Sometimes I have to empty out
To let go, dump all I've learned
Perceptions, truths, ways of being
From others
All out of love
To give me ways to learn
... and I have

Sometimes I have to empty out
Too much noise, it's too loud
From my cloud I empty out
It falls like rain
Gently to the ground

The thing about being empty
Is, now room I have plenty
Space for my soul to reside
Infinite, I am inside

It can be scary to let go
But once cleared
The garden
Has magnificent potential

Seeds I sow
Dreams, ways to flow
Uncertain, I don't know

The regeneration of emptying out
Those old ways of being
Fall as rain from the cloud
And water my future
On the ground

EMPTY SPACE

Empty space
Open space
Allowing new
Yet, no need to chase

Empty isn't loss

Fresh sown ground
A potential
Open space
To plant a new garden

Chapters in life end
Empty space now

Until the calling
We wait in silence
Without a sound

Shedding skins, letting go
Not forcing once passioned doings
Allowing a new flow
For new dreams to grow

Now I may not know
The mystery of my soul's dream
I can follow the flowers
Mysterious cosmic showers
A greater path before me

Abounds

SLOW LIFE

I realize I need a slow life
And I mean slow
Taking an hour to eat a plate of fruit
Allows my body to heal and grow

I realize I need a slow life
One that requires less work days
For working too much sends my body reeling
Into an endless vortex of strife

I realize I need a slow life
To cherish each moment
Each day
Water my garden
Say hello to each plant
Time to give the bees a drink
Trellis my tomatoes just right

I realize I need a slow life
To watch the eastern phoebes
In the bird house next door
Build a nest, a family
Slowly growing
By each bit of food
They're sharing
To watch the young'ins fly away
New life, from them
Will splay

I realize I need a slow life
To actually realize I'm alive
That I indeed am physical
Yet a spirit I reside
Inside

OUT MY BACK DOOR

The mourning dove coos
Breaking my tradesman blues
Out my backdoor stoop
Will the neighbors snoop?

Orange orioles cheep
High up in the red pine
Choke cherries flutter
In the wind, new limbs
Pin oak pushes off the
Crusty leaves from yesteryear
Easy to let go when spring is here

The weathered brown ladder
Taken to the dump a time or two
Only to be reused by some
Yellow painter, or patter up to the top bunk
Car doors slamming, generator a-whirring
Childish banter in old skins like leather
We're all weathered here
Big hearts with nothing left to fear

This noisy silence somehow
Breaks the silence in my life
Being so exposed, so open
Is the last spell to be broken

The white pine remains
In my vision out the pane
Two rotting stumps
What to do with such things?
A young mulberry perhaps?
On the edge of a young currant grove
It's so lovely to meet my neighbors
A tiny little forest I can thwart
Maybe I don't need so much after all
My mind, heart, & feet
Can take me to neat places
With all too familiar nature faces

MAGIC

Where within you
Does the magic inside
Reside?

SOONER

I just might get there sooner than I realize
Life unfolding before my very eyes

THE PATH

Keep moving forward
And rest when you need to
The fire within you
Is your hidden truth

Ashley Lynn

ADAPTING

Life often asks us to adapt

If we're not willing to morph
We can become stagnant
Fall behind

Some things are worth holding onto
But if they stifle your growth

It is okay to

G e n t l y

L e t

G o

To grow

LIBERATION

Liberation is

Living as a nobody
Feeling complete in the soul
Being free and full
Living by my ideals
Breaking all "shoulds"
Coulds
Woulds
And being free as a bird

Walking barefoot on Earth
Making love passionately
And knowing
My soul is eternal
And not bound here
Knowing
I get to go home after this
Whether back to the sun in the sky
A watery planet, the dog's eye
Or an ancient land with
Lizards in the sky

Zooming out
Is liberation
That this one life
Isn't the destination

END HERE

During my Dark Night, I faced the grief of losing important people in my life and parts of myself that I loved and left behind to take on the spiritual persona I projected online.

Having relationships in person was difficult for me during the writing of these poems because I tried to be myself and my internet self at the same time. My online persona and who I was in reality didn't mesh, like oil and water, and I felt insecure and isolated from others. Some of my poems express this part of the journey.

Other poems are about society and the systems we have in place. I shared my frustrations and concerns with where we're headed from the perspective of a nature lover who refuses to give my body and soul to corporate land.

Throughout the process of writing and editing this collection, I changed so much as a person. I matured. I saw that people, online and in person, aren't always who they say they are. I felt betrayed. I gave up on several mindsets that I took on.

Some of the philosophies and mindsets I wrote about I don't believe in anymore. Yet, there are some that still hold true to me.

As a hungry truth seeker, I consider the truth behind most of what I look into and study. For most of my twenties, I was enthralled in metaphysics and spirituality, fooled by flattery, repetitive flowery language, and false hope. I was looking for something, *anything* to help me feel better living in a world I felt out of place in. Society was broken in my eyes and I didn't want to be a part of it.

I went deep into internet culture, morphed by many influencers because I thought they would help me become a better person. I thought being eco-conscious and spiritually aware was "the way" and strongly believed in "be the change you wish to see in the world."

The internet became my life. I had a platform where I shared the "spiritual truths" I lived by along with my art & writing revealing a fantasy world meant to be taken as truth. This was my online persona, a cosmically aware person resonating in a different dimension.

I lived and breathed the ways of internet culture and my online personality until I couldn't anymore. It broke me because I lived against my natural state of being. The Crisis began here.

Because I was vulnerable, I involved myself with the new age/spirituality community on the internet. My childhood was traumatic and I went through years of hardship and adversity afterwards. I needed some way to make sense of it all, to have some hope that things would get better.

I didn't realize the new age/spirituality community online was one of the *causes* of my hardships, influencing me to make choices in ways outside of logic and the reality of the world we live in. I take full responsibility for my actions, it was my choice to think and be this way. And I don't regret any part of my past, it made me who I am today.

Once I realized I was out in the middle of space isolating myself from my family, friends, and people of the world, I felt something was wrong and began my decent back into normalcy.

I gave up my old platform, persona, and creativity for months into years. It was only when I felt *another* part of me missing that I decided to get back into my creative outlets to try again, but this time as myself with no masks or "teachings" to preach.

As an artist, writer, and musician, it occurred to me that if I want to earn money from my work then I must have a presence online, especially social media. Much of my pain came from the marketing aspect of art, having to post to a social media site to get seen.

Writing and editing this collection was a personal journey I took to shed my old self. The significance of the cicada on the cover is just that - emerging as a bright new being from a brown shell buried in the earth. When a cicada molts its previous form, it emerges turquoise and light green before changing into its adulthood colors.

Publishing this book is my way of helping the world - with my words, misery, emotions. To show others that our emotions, no matter what they are, can be felt and are a part of the human experience. All emotions are valid. It's okay to give them a voice because listening, truly listening, is a beautiful way to turn shadows into light. The darkness within can only be free if we let it be seen.

ACKNOWLEDGEMENTS

This poetry collection in your hands wouldn't have been possible without beautiful people who've helped me complete it. You all have restored my faith in humanity, helped me reconnect with others after this difficult time in my life. Your kindness and support kept me going when I was about to give up on my writing dreams. Thank you!

To my editor Dakota Reed who received this collection in its initial mess - thank you for giving me constructive feedback and advice on how to improve it as gently as you did. The bits of action steps you gave me catapulted this project into a state that I felt comfortable sharing with others.

To my beta readers - thank you for giving my book a chance without knowing who I am. Reading my collection in your spare time and giving me feedback is such a gift to have as a writer. Thank you for catching the typos, helping me organize the poems, sharing your thoughts about your favorite poems and how they remind you of the grieving process. Every piece of feedback you gave was put into the final copy of the book and it is complete because of your help! I appreciate each and every one of you for sharing a piece of your heart with me.

To all my ARC readers - thank you for being some of the first to read the collection in its polished state and for leaving your reviews on your favorite sites. Because of you, this book can find others who feel like they don't belong in society and give them a reason to try. Thank you for your help in making launching a book easier.

To my sister - thank you for chatting with me every week during the hardest part of the journey of finishing this book while reconnecting with myself. You were my friend while processing all of the shadows, lending an ear to listen and being the first person to read the book. Your initial thoughts of the poems made me realize that they weren't *that bad* and it was worth finishing the book to put out into the world. Thank you for your encouragement and love for me during such a hard time in my life.

And the rest of my family - I'm grateful for your love and support when I was coming back down to earth and figuring myself out again. You gave me space, while also being family I could rely on. Mom, for your unconditional love and respect for the person I've become, my brother for fun, humor and someone I look up to, and my other sister for her sweetness and eagerness to offer helpful solutions to whatever comes up. I'm so lucky to have you as my family!

Many thanks to the friends I made at the organic farm I worked at this summer. You didn't intentionally do anything for me, but you restored my faith in humanity with your natural kindness and wholesomeness. You made me feel like I belonged somewhere and for once in my life, I want to come back and continue to be a part of the community. Thank you for the lighthearted and deep conversations shared while pulling weeds, harvesting vegetables, and packing food for others. I love you guys and can't wait to see you soon.

Austin, I'm so grateful for you standing by my side through the good and the bad times. During my "ither days," you stuck around even though I was delusional and confused about a lot of things. Traveling along the journey of life with you has been a rollercoaster, but I would't want to do it with anyone else. Thank you for being an ear to listen to me and give me insights when I talk about my creative work... relentlessly.

A shoutout to my favorite band, Peach Pit. Your music and art showed me that feeling melancholy, sad, and lonely is normal and more than okay. You guys gave me permission to express myself through these poems and the courage to create this book. Thank you for making kick ass music that helped me get through the hard times in life.

Lastly, thank you to my readers and supporters of my poetry and Adventures Across. I started this journey seven years ago and some of you have been here the entire time, watching me morph and change as I figure out this whole "creative career" thing. I'm grateful for you, your interest in me and what I'm creating!

WHAT DID YOU THINK ABOUT THIS BOOK…?

Would you consider leaving a review on Goodreads, Amazon, or your favorite social media site?

You can find the Amazon page here:

https://a.co/d/cl2xpYw

Goodreads here:
https://www.goodreads.com/book/show/216380541-befriending-shadows

And if you share on social media, feel free to tag me:

Instagram: @ashleylynn.writes

YouTube: @asterlately

Pinterest: @ashleylynnwrites

Tumblr: @ashleylynnwrites

Find Ashley in other places:

Medium: https://medium.com/asterlately

In the Pursuit of Something Real (newsletter): https://adventuresacross.substack.com/

Poetry Newsletter: https://ashleylynnwrites.substack.com/

Art Store: https://ko-fi.com/asterlately

Instagram: https://instagram.com/ashleylynn.writes

Adventure Videos: https://youtube.com/@adventuresacross

Art Videos: https://youtube.com/@asterlately

Contact:
Email: ashleylynn.writes@proton.me

About Adventures Across Press: https://medium.com/@asterlately/about-adventures-across-press-f5c5618b64be

Ashley Lynn is a poet, writer, artist, and musician. She calls a camper her home and migrates with the seasons. Her work is inspired by her journey as an artist, as well as nature, adventure, the spirit, and living alternatively. Ashley runs multiple blogs about being a "professional hobbyist" and exploring the planet (Aster Lately); and connecting with our soul through nature and creativity (In the Pursuit of Something Real). When she isn't creating or writing, she is a window washer and an organic farm hand.

Other Works by Ashley Lynn:

A Year Against the Rain - Lessons Learned Living Off Grid on the Oregon Coast

Morning Motivations - Uplifting Poetry to Start Your Day

The Adventures Across Guided Journal (discontinued)

Find Me in the Forest - Poems & Ponderings of Nature, Consciousness, & Self

www.ingramcontent.com/pod-product-compliance
Lightning Source LLC
Chambersburg PA
CBHW030831090426
42737CB00009B/959